Taking Turns

Taking Turns

POETRY TO SHARE

Collected by **Bernice Wolman**
Illustrated by **Catherine Stock**

ATHENEUM 1992 NEW YORK

Maxwell Macmillan Canada · Toronto
Maxwell Macmillan International
New York · Oxford · Singapore · Sydney

For Ted
—B. W.

For Bertrand
—C. S.

Library of Congress Cataloging-in-Publication Data. Taking turns: poetry to
share / collected by Bernice Wolman. p.   cm. Summary: Pairs of poems—one
simpler, one more sophisticated —provide opportunities for parent and child to read
aloud together on such themes as rain, horses, the wind, loneliness, and books
themselves. ISBN 0-689-31677-1. 1. Children's poetry, American. 2. Children's
poetry, English. [1. Poetry—Collections.] I. Wolman, Bernice. PS586.3.T26 1992
821.008'09282—dc20 90-46533 CIP AC

Contents

Who Has Seen the Wind?

Who has seen the wind?
  Neither I nor you:
But when the leaves hang trembling
  The wind is passing through.

Who has seen the wind?
  Neither you nor I:
But when the trees bow down their heads
  The wind is passing by.

Christina Rossetti

Little Wind

Little wind, blow on the hill-top,
 Little wind, blow down the plain;
Little wind, blow up the sunshine,
 Little wind, blow off the rain.

Kate Greenaway

April Rain Song

Let the rain kiss you.
Let the rain beat upon your head with silver liquid drops.
Let the rain sing you a lullaby.

The rain makes still pools on the sidewalk.
The rain makes running pools in the gutter.
The rain plays a little sleep-song on our roof at night—

And I love the rain.

Langston Hughes

Rain

The rain is raining all around
It falls on field and tree,
It rains on the umbrellas here,
And on the ships at sea.

Robert Louis Stevenson

All of a Sudden

Galloping galloping galloping galloping,
The horses gallop along the meadows,
Click on the rocks and soft on
    the grasses,
Racing the clouds and the clouds'
    long shadows.

They run as the wind runs, they
    run like the shadows;
From their hoofs the dust drifts
    away in a haze.
Galloping galloping galloping galloping—
All of a sudden, they stop to graze!

Elizabeth Coatsworth

The Horses

Red horse,
Roan horse,
Black horse,
And white,
Feeding all together in the green
    summer light.

White horse,
Black horse,
Spotted horse,
And gray,
I wish that I were off with you,
    far, far away!

Elizabeth Coatsworth

A Calendar

January brings the snow,
Makes our feet and fingers glow.

February brings the rain,
Thaws the frozen lake again.

March brings breezes, loud and shrill,
To stir the dancing daffodil.

April brings the primrose sweet,
Scatters daisies at our feet.

May brings flocks of pretty lambs
Skipping by their fleecy dams.

June brings tulips, lilies, roses,
Fills the children's hands with posies.

Hot July brings cooling showers,
Apricots, and gillyflowers.

August brings the sheaves of corn,
Then the harvest home is borne.

Warm September brings the fruit;
Sportsmen then begin to shoot.

Fresh October brings the pheasant;
Then to gather nuts is pleasant.

Dull November brings the blast;
Then the leaves are whirling fast.

Chill December brings the sleet,
Blazing fire, and Christmas treat.

Sara Coleridge

The Months

January snowy,
    February flowy,
        March blowy;

April showery,
    May flowery,
        June bowery;

July moppy,
    August croppy,
        September poppy;

October breezy,
    November wheezy,
        December freezy.

      Richard B. Sheridan

Velvet Shoes

Let us walk in the white snow
   In a soundless space;
With footsteps quiet and slow,
   At a tranquil pace,
    Under veils of white lace.

I shall go shod in silk,
   And you in wool,
White as a white cow's milk,
   More beautiful
    Than the breast of a gull.

We shall walk through the still town
   In a windless peace;
We shall step upon white down,
   Upon silver fleece,
    Upon softer than these.

We shall walk in velvet shoes;
   Wherever we go
Silence will fall like dews
   On white silence below.
    We shall walk in the snow.

Elinor Wylie

Snow

Snow
Snow
Lots of snow
Everywhere we look and everywhere we go
Snow in the sandbox
Snow on the slide
Snow on the bicycle
Left outside
Snow on the steps
And snow on my feet
Snow on the sidewalk
Snow on the sidewalk
Snow on the sidewalk
Down the street.

Mary Ann Hoberman

The Skaters

Black swallows swooping or gliding
In a flurry of entangled loops and curves;
The skaters skim over the frozen river.
And the grinding click of their skates
    as they impinge upon the surface,
Is like the brushing together
    of thin wing-tips of silver.

John Gould Fletcher

Ice Skating

Higher and higher
I glide in the sky,
My feet flashing silver,
A star in each eye.
With wind at my back
I can float, I can soar.
The earth cannot hold me
In place anymore.

Sandra Liatsos

Catalog

Cats sleep fat and walk thin.
Cats, when they sleep, slump;
When they wake, pull in—
And where the plump's been
There's skin.
Cats walk thin.

Cats sleep fat.
They spread comfort beneath them
Like a good mat,
As if they picked the place
And then sat.
You walk around one
As if he were the City Hall
After that.

When everyone else is just ready to go out,
The cat is just ready to come in.
He's not where he's been.
Cats sleep fat and walk thin.

Rosalie Moore

My Kitten

Kitten, my kitten,
   Soft and dear,
I am so glad
   That we are here
Sitting together
   Just us two
You loving me
   And me loving you.

Marchette Chute

19

The Mouse

I hear a mouse
Bitterly complaining
In a crack of moonlight
Aslant on the floor—

'Little I ask
And that little is not granted.
There are few crumbs
In this world any more.

'The breadbox is tin
And I cannot get in.

'The jam's in a jar
My teeth cannot mar.

'The cheese sits by itself
On the pantry shelf.

'All night I run
Searching and seeking.
All night I run
About on the floor.

'Moonlight is there
And a bare place for dancing,
But no little feast
Is spread any more.'

Elizabeth Coatsworth

Mice

I think mice
Are rather nice.

Their tails are long,
Their faces small,
They haven't any
Chins at all.
Their ears are pink,
Their teeth are white,
They run about
The house at night.
They nibble things
They shouldn't touch
And no one seems
To like them much.

But I think mice
Are nice.

Rose Fyleman

21

I Can Fly

I can fly, of course,
Very low,
Not fast,
Rather slow.
I spread my arms
Like wings,
Lean on the wind,
And my body zings
About.
Nothing showy—
A few loops
And turns—
But for the most
Part,
I just coast.

However,
Since people are prone
To talk about
It,
I generally prefer,
Unless I am alone,
Just to walk about.

Felice Holman

Up in the Air

Zooming across the sky,
Like a great bird you fly,
　　Airplane
　　Silvery white
　　In the light.

Turning and twisting in air,
When shall I ever be there,
　　Airplane,
　　Piloting you
　　Far in the blue?

James S. Tippett

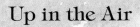

Living Tenderly

My body a rounded stone
with a pattern of smooth seams.
My head a short snake,
retractive, projective.
My legs come out of their sleeves
or shrink within,
and so does my chin.
My eyelids are quick clamps.

My back is my roof.
I am always at home.
I travel where my house walks.
It is a smooth stone.

It floats within the lake,
or rests in the dust.
My flesh lives tenderly
inside its bone.

                                May Swenson

The Little Turtle

There was a little turtle.
He lived in a box.
He swam in a puddle.
He climbed on the rocks.

He snapped at a mosquito.
He snapped at a flea.
He snapped at a minnow.
And he snapped at me.

He caught the mosquito.
He caught the flea.
He caught the minnow.
But he didn't catch me.

Vachel Lindsay

Growing Smiles

A smile is quite a funny thing,
It wrinkles up your face,
And when it's gone, you never find
Its secret hiding place.

But far more wonderful it is
To see what smiles can do;
You smile at one, he smiles at you,
And so one smile makes two.

He smiles at someone since you smiled,
And then that one smiles back;
And that one smiles, until in truth
You fail in keeping track.

Now since a smile can do great good
By cheering hearts of care,
Let's smile and smile, and not forget
That smiles go everywhere!

Unknown

26

People

Some people talk and talk
and never say a thing.
Some people look at you
and birds begin to sing.

Some people laugh and laugh
and yet you want to cry.
Some people touch your hand
and music fills the sky.

Charlotte Zolotow

Loneliness

Still, still, stillness
In my head, in my heart.
> *Is there anyone there?*
> *Is there anyone there?*

The world's outside
And I want to be a part.
> *Is there anyone there?*
> *Is there anyone there?*

There's a coldness inside,
It's so very wintery.
I'm here. *Here* I am,
Alone and lonely.
> *Is there anyone there?*
> *Is there anyone there?*
> *For me?*

Felice Holman

Hope

Sometimes when I'm lonely,
Don't know why,
Keep thinkin' I won't be lonely
By and by.

Langston Hughes

29

Who Hath a Book

Who hath a book
  Hath friends at hand,
And gold and gear
  At his command;
And rich estates,
  If he but look,
Are held by him
  Who hath a book.

Who hath a book
  Hath but to read
And he may be
  A king, indeed.
His kingdom is
  His inglenook—
All this is his
  Who hath a book.

Wilbur D. Nesbit

Books to the Ceiling

Books to the ceiling, books to the sky.
My piles of books are a mile high.
How I love them!
How I need them!
I'll have a long beard by the time I read them.

Arnold Lobel

For reprint permission grateful acknowledgment is made to:

Coward-McCann, Inc., for "The Mouse" from COMPASS ROSE by Elizabeth
Coatsworth, copyright © 1929 by Coward-McCann, Inc. Copyright renewed
© 1957 by Elizabeth Coatsworth.

Doubleday, a division of Bantam Doubleday Dell Publishing Group, Inc., for
"Mice" from FIFTY-ONE NEW NURSERY RHYMES by Rose Fyleman, copyright © 1931, 1932 by Doubleday.

Greenwillow Books, a division of William Morrow & Company, for "Books to the
Ceiling" from WHISKERS & RHYMES by Arnold Lobel. Text copyright © 1985
by Arnold Lobel.

Grosset & Dunlap, Inc., for "The Horses" and "All of a Sudden" from THE
SPARROW BUSH, copyright © 1966 by Grosset & Dunlap.

HarperCollins Publishers for "Up in the Air" from CRICKETY CRICKET! THE
BEST LOVED POEMS OF JAMES TIPPET. Copyright © 1933, "A World to Know."
Renewed text copyright © 1973, Martha K. Tippett, and "People" from ALL
THAT SUNLIGHT by Charlotte Zolotow.

Felice Holman for "Loneliness" © 1987 from I LIKE YOU IF YOU LIKE ME,
reprinted by permission of Felice Holman, the copyright owner, and for "I
Can Fly" from AT THE TOP OF MY VOICE. Reprinted by permission of Felice
Holman, the copyright owner, and Charles Scribner's Sons (1970).

Alfred A. Knopf, Inc., for "April Rain Song" by Langston Hughes, reprinted from
THE DREAM KEEPER AND OTHER POEMS by Langston Hughes, copyright
© 1932 by Alfred A. Knopf, Inc., and renewed 1960 by Langston Hughes; and
for "Velvet Shoes" by Elinor Wylie from COLLECTED POEMS OF ELINOR
WYLIE, copyright © 1921 by Alfred A. Knopf, Inc., and renewed 1949 by
William Rose Benét.

Sandra Liatsos for "Ice Skating." Used by permission of the author, who controls
all rights. First appeared in the "Instructor Magazine" and Harper & Row's
"Surprises." Copyright © 1984.

Gina Maccoby Literary Agency for "Snow" from YELLOW BUTTER PURPLE
JELLY RED JAM BLACK BREAD. Copyright © 1981 by Mary Ann Hoberman.

The New Yorker Magazine, Inc., for portions of "Catalog" by Rosalie Moore,
© 1940, 1968, The New Yorker Magazine, Inc.

Harold Ober Associates, Inc., for "Hope" from SELECTED POEMS © 1959 by
Langston Hughes. Copyright renewed 1987 by George Houston Bass.

Mary Chute Smith, copyright owner for "My Kitten" from RHYMES ABOUT US,
copyright © 1974 by Marchette Chute.

The Literary Estate of May Swenson for "Living Tenderly" © 1963, used with
permission.